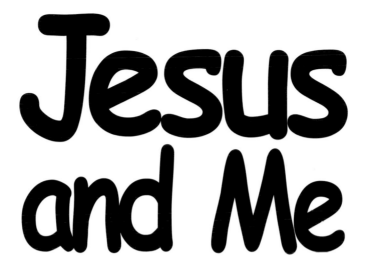

Jesus and Me

FIVE-MINUTE VIRTUES TO GROW ON
V. GILBERT BEERS
Illustrated by Tony Kenyon

HARVEST
HOUSE
PUBLISHERS
Eugene, Oregon 97402

Text © 1998 V. Gilbert Beers
This edition © 1998 Angus Hudson Ltd/
Tim Dowley & Peter Wyart trading as
Three's Company

Designed by Peter Wyart
Three's Company

Published in the U.S.A. by
Harvest House Publishers
Eugene, Oregon 97402

ISBN 1-56507-753-9

Worldwide coedition organized and
produced by
Angus Hudson Ltd,
Concorde House, Grenville Place,
Mill Hill, London NW7 3SA, England
Tel: +44 181 959 3668
Fax +44 181 959 3678

Printed in Singapore

98 99 00 01 02 03/9 8 7 6 5 4 3 2 1

For Parents and Teachers

When I was a boy on an Illinois farm, there was something special about a summer evening. With dinner and dishwashing done, the entire family went to the front porch and talked the evening away. That was another era. When our children were in their growing-up years, we didn't have entire evenings to talk. They were busy in orchestras, little leagues, doing homework, and a dozen other things. Our evenings were filled with activity too.

The old farmhouse is gone and with it has passed a wonderful family experience. We live in another time now, when few people could hope to spend entire evenings talking as a family.

But with our children we have had hundreds of little talks, some lasting only five or ten minutes, and some longer. We have talked of many things—of the days when Indians lived in our backyard, of hurts and problems that our children brought home from school, and of all the little things they encountered on their pilgrimages through life. The most special times have been our little talks about God and where He fits into their lives and ours.

Consistently through the years, my wife, Arlie, brought out the storybooks before bedtime and read with drama and flourish to our wide-eyed children. It was an everyday sight to see her sitting there with children wrapped around her as she and they literally wore the covers off favorite books. Of course, this reading always prompted little talks, too.

Arlie and I have deliberately looked for every excuse we could find to stop and have a little talk with our children. One-on-one times were the best, because then we could really get into the child's head and heart. We've had little talks sprawled on the floor, draped over a sofa, sitting on a log in the woods, hiking a trail, in a canoe, and at a dozen other favorite haunts. Little talks were almost never planned—they just happened. Yet in these wonderful, brief encounters we cultivated lasting friendships with our children. Now they are grown, and they are truly our best friends. And often they are our most honest counselors.

Frequently parents or teachers think a good talk must be a long talk. More often the opposite is true—five-minute talks can bear wonderful fruit. The prerequisite is that during those five minutes you must truly be with your child and not let your heart or mind be elsewhere. If you talk grudgingly, you will not talk productively.

In this book you will find little talks that will take from five minutes to as long as you want to talk. If you read one each day with your child, and talk about it, you will see wonderful things begin to happen in your relationship. It's a five-minute lifebuilding exercise, and it will be pure fun too.

These are little talks about great truths, but great truths made simple. In a very real sense they involve you in a special time with your child and God. Your child learns that these times for little talks are times of delight when he or she will get to know you and God a little better each day.

Younger children will also enjoy reading this book, for it is written in a simple style designed to make reading easy. When they do, these everyday situations will encourage them to have little talks with God or you.

Invest in time with your child each day. There is no more rewarding investment to be made. The dividends are wonderful, and they are eternal.

V. Gilbert Beers

Contents

A Smiling *Face*

Carol looked at the envelope that Mother had received in the mail. On the back was a big yellow dot with a smiling face on it.

"Why do people put smiling faces on envelopes?" Carol asked Mother.

A Little Talk about *Cheerfulness*

1. Have you seen those little yellow smiling faces? Why do you think someone puts one on an envelope?

2. Would you rather see a sad face or a smiling face? Why?

3. What do you think Mother will tell Carol?

A LITTLE TALK about
Jesus and You

1. Why should Christians have smiling faces? Why are we so happy?

2. Have you smiled for Jesus today? Do you look happy and smile because you love Him?

Bible Reading: Proverbs 15:13,15,30.

Bible Truth: A cheerful look brings joy to those who see you (Proverbs 15:30).

Prayer: Dear Jesus, as I look at this little yellow smiling face, help me remember to show others how cheerful I am. When someone wants to know why, help me to tell them about You. Amen.

Sharing Is *Fun*

Two boys went to school one day. One forgot his lunch, so he had nothing to eat. The other boy brought his lunch. He had two sandwiches, an apple, a pear, and four cookies.

At lunchtime the first boy stayed behind in the classroom to read a book. The second boy headed toward the lunchroom to eat his food.

A Little Talk about *Sharing*

1. What did the first boy have to eat for lunch? What did the second boy have to eat for lunch?

2. If you were the boy with the lunch, what would you do about the other boy without a lunch?

When the boy with the lunch saw his friend stay in the classroom, he came back to talk with him. Then he learned that his friend had forgotten his lunch.

So the boy who had his lunch shared. He had a pear, one sandwich, and two cookies. The boy who forgot his lunch had an apple, one sandwich, and two cookies. And both boys had a happy time eating together.

A LITTLE TALK about
Jesus and You

1. Why do you think the boy who forgot his lunch was happy as he ate? Why do you think the boy who remembered his lunch was happy while he ate?

2. Why do you think Jesus was happy to watch the two boys eat their lunch?

Bible Reading: Matthew 6:2-4.

Bible Truth: Share with God's people who have need (Romans 12:13).

Prayer: You have shared so much with me, dear Jesus. Help me to share happily with others so that I may please You and be like You. Amen.

Listen!

Grandpa was reading his newspaper, as grandpas often do. But Fred wanted to ask some questions, as boys often do when grandpas are reading their newspapers.

When Fred asked his first question, Grandpa mumbled something that sounded like "ummph." When Fred asked his second question, Grandpa grunted a little. It sounded a little like "um hum." And when Fred asked his third question, Grandpa was so interested in his reading that he didn't even answer.

"Are you listening?" Fred asked Grandpa.

A Little Talk about
Listening

1. Do you think Grandpa was listening? Why not?

2. What do you think Fred would like Grandpa to do? What would you do if you were Grandpa?

Grandpa put down his newspaper. "What did you say?" he asked Fred.

"I asked if you were listening," Fred replied.

"I'm sorry," said Grandpa. "I was not listening. I let the newspaper talk louder than you. Please ask your questions again, and this time I will listen carefully."

A LITTLE TALK about
Jesus and You

1. How often does Jesus listen when you talk to Him? How often would you like Him to listen? Why?

2. Why do you think listening pleases Jesus? How does listening help other people know what Jesus is like? Can we tell others that Jesus listens if we, who are His friends, don't listen?

Bible Reading: Psalm 34:4-6.

Bible Truth: God said, "While they are still speaking I will hear" (Isaiah 65:24).

Prayer: Thank You, Lord, for listening at all times. Thank You for never going to sleep or doing something else while I talk with You. Amen.

Thanking
God

"I earned the money for this food," a man said. "Why should I thank God for it?"

"I bought this food at the grocery store," a woman said. "Why should I thank God for it?"

"I worked hard to plant my garden and gather the things that grew there," said another man. "Why should I thank God for them?"

"Mother made dinner for me tonight," a boy said. "Why should I thank God for it?"

A Little Talk about
Being Thankful

1. What would you say to each of these people? Why should they thank God for their food?

2. Who earned the money for your food? Have you thanked Mother or Father for that? Who cooks your food for you? Have you thanked Mother or Father for that? Who shopped at the grocery store for your food? Have you thanked Mother or Father for that?

3. Why should you thank God for your food?

Look through your pantry or cabinet where you store your food. Ask Mother to do this with you. Try to find a food that God did not cause to grow.

Every kind of fruit and vegetable needed God's warm sunshine and rain to grow. Every kind of animal needed green grass or grain to eat. Green grass and grain need God's sunshine and rain. You will not find one food that didn't need God to help it grow. Is that why we should thank Him for food?

A LITTLE TALK about
God and You

1. Did you find any food that didn't need God to help it grow? All food was created by God and needed His sunshine or rain.

2. Who made you? Can you stay alive long without food? Who made your food? Have you thanked God today for your food? Perhaps you would like to do that now.

3. Have you thanked Mother and Father for buying and cooking food for you? Perhaps you would like to do that now also.

Bible Reading: Genesis 1:29,30.

Bible Truth: Give us each day our food for that day (Luke 11:3).

Prayer: Thank You, Lord, for food to eat. Thank You for Mother and Father, who buy and cook the food that You have made. Amen.

Tall Tales

Brian was telling some friends a tall tale. It just wasn't true. Some friends laughed and said he was fibbing. Some other friends said he was lying.

Brian was trying to make his friends think he did something he didn't do. Then his friends would think he was very important. Do you think tall tales work this way?

A Little Talk about
Lying

1. What was Brian trying to do? Would you say he was fibbing, telling a tall tale, or lying?

2. Have you heard a friend tell a lie? How did you feel when you heard this? Have you ever told a lie? How do you think other people felt when they heard you? How did you feel?

Brian may think his friends will like him better when he tells his tall tale. But they won't. They will like him less. They will know that he is lying. It's hard to think good things about a person who is lying, isn't it?

That is something for you and me to remember the next time we want to tell a tall tale.

A Little Talk about
Jesus and You

1. Do you think Jesus would ever lie about anything? Why not?

2. Do you think Jesus' friends should ever lie about anything? Why not?

3. What does Jesus think when His friends tell a lie? Do you think He is ashamed of them?

Bible Reading: Proverbs 6:16-19.

Bible Truth: The Lord hates lying lips, but loves people who tell the truth (Proverbs 12:22).

Prayer: Lord, remind me to tell the truth so that You will never be ashamed of me and so that people can trust me. Amen.

Forgiving
Debts

When Gregg went on a field trip with his class he borrowed a dollar from one of his friends for some ice cream. He borrowed two dollars from another friend for some souvenirs. And he borrowed two dollars from still another friend for a poster. Another friend lent him a dollar for popcorn.

On the way home Gregg began to add up how much he owed. He could hardly believe it! He owed six dollars to his four friends! How could he ever pay back all that money?

When Gregg got home he looked so worried that Father asked him about it. Then Gregg told Father what had happened. He told Father how sorry he was that he had done this.

A Little Talk about
Debts

1. What did Gregg do that was foolish? How do you know he was sorry that he had done this?

2. If you were Gregg's father, what would you say to him now? What would you do?

"I will pay your debts for you this time," said Father, "just as Jesus paid my debts for me."

"Did you borrow too much money from someone?" Gregg asked.

Father smiled. "No, not money," he said. "When we sin, we get into debt. We can never pay for all our sins. But Jesus said that He would pay my debts for me. I was sorry for those debts and asked Him to pay for them—and He did."

Have you asked Jesus to pay your sin debts for you?

A LITTLE TALK about
Jesus and You

1. What kind of debts did Father pay for Gregg? What kind of debts did Jesus pay for Father?

2. Have you asked Jesus to forgive you and be your Savior? When you do, He forgives the debts you have because of sin just like He did for Gregg's father.

Bible Reading: Matthew 6:9-15.

Bible Truth: Jesus will forgive us, just as we forgive others (Matthew 6:12).

Prayer: Dear Jesus, forgive me for the wrong things I have done. Remind me to live for You the way You want me to. Amen.

Do You Like to
Obey?

"Sit!" Cindy said to her dog Lance. But Lance looked up with sleepy eyes and rolled over.

"Mother," said Cindy, "Lance will not obey me. He should be ashamed of himself."

"This reminds me of dinnertime last night," said Mother with a smile. "I called and called, but a girl named Cindy didn't come."

Cindy looked down at the floor. "I'm sorry," she said. "It is important to obey, isn't it?"

A Little Talk about
Obeying

1. What did Lance do that Cindy didn't like? Why was Cindy angry?

2. What had Cindy done that was like Lance? What do you think Mother should tell Cindy about this?

"Why do you want Lance to obey you?" asked Mother.

Cindy thought for a minute. "What if I knew something is about to hurt Lance? He could get hurt if he doesn't obey me," said Cindy.

"Any other reason?" Mother asked.

"What if I had something good for him, like a bone?" said Cindy. "If he doesn't obey me when I call, he won't get it."

"Those are two good reasons," said Mother. "And they are two good reasons for boys and girls to obey their parents and Jesus."

"I promise that I will try to obey you and Jesus from now on," said Cindy. "And I'm glad Lance didn't obey today so we could have this little talk."

A LITTLE TALK about
Jesus and You

1. What did Cindy learn about obeying? What are two good reasons to obey parents and Jesus?

2. Jesus gave another reason for obeying. Look at the Bible Truth below.

Bible Reading: John 14:23,24.

Bible Truth: Jesus said, "If you love me, obey what I say" (John 14:15).

Prayer: Jesus, I'm glad that I can talk with You and be Your friend. I'm glad that I can obey You, because I know that You will always help me do what is right. Amen.

Is Cheating Worth It?

Dean scratched his head and rubbed his nose. But he just couldn't remember the answer. Then he looked at Faith. She had already written her answer, and it was sure to be right. Faith was always right on things like this. All Dean had to do was move just a little closer and peek over Faith's shoulder.

Dean started to look. Then something inside him nudged him back. He started to look again. But he didn't feel good about it.

A Little Talk about
Cheating

1. Why do you think Dean is not sure about cheating? Why doesn't he just go ahead and do it?

2. How do you think Dean will feel the next day if he cheats on this test? How would you feel?

"I won't do it," said Dean. "I will feel terrible if I do. And I know that Jesus will not be pleased."

So Dean put down the best answer he could. When he did, it seemed like it was the right one.

"Even if it isn't the right answer, I've done the right thing," Dean thought.

Do you think Dean did the right thing?

A LITTLE TALK about
Jesus and You

1. Do you think Jesus would have been pleased if Dean had cheated? Why?

2. Do you think Jesus is pleased with the way Dean did this? Why? What would you like to say to Dean now?

Bible Reading: Philippians 4:8,9.

Bible Truth: Think about things that are true, great, right, pure, and lovely (Philippians 4:8).

Prayer: Dear Jesus, teach me not to cheat, for I know that I will be cheating myself most of all. Amen.

A Comforting
Voice

Andrea sat up in bed and looked at the soft light in the hallway. She saw a shadow of a person coming toward her door. The shadow looked big and dark. Suddenly Andrea was afraid. She began to cry.

A Little Talk about Being
Afraid

1. What did Andrea see? Why is she so afraid?

2. What do you think is making that shadow? What would you like to say to Andrea?

"Don't cry, Andrea," a voice said softly. "It's only me."

Andrea stopped crying as soon as she heard her big sister's voice. When her big sister came into the room, Andrea put her arms around her and hugged her tight.

A LITTLE TALK about
Jesus and You

1. Are you ever afraid of the shadows of the trees or bushes at night?

2. You wouldn't be afraid if Jesus whispered softly to you, would you? You wouldn't be afraid if He put His arms around you and hugged you, right?

Bible Reading: John 10:14-16.

Bible Truth: Jesus' friends follow Him because they know His voice (John 10:4).

Prayer: Dear Jesus, when I am afraid, please be with me. Then I will not be afraid anymore. Amen.

How Should *We Give?*

Two boys gave their mother birthday gifts. One boy spent all his money and bought his mother a beautiful gift, but he played with his friends all day. The other boy didn't have any money, but he made a birthday card for his mother. On the card he told her what a wonderful mother she was and how much he loved her. Then he spent most of the day helping his mother and doing things she liked to do.

A Little Talk about *Giving*

1. Which gift was better? Which gift do you like better?

2. Do the best gifts cost the most money? What kind of gifts are best?

3. Will you remember this the next time your mother or father has a special day?

The best gifts are not things. Almost anyone can buy things and give them away. The best gifts are yourself and your love. Nobody else can give that.

What if the gifts were from Mother or Father? Would you rather have your parents be with you on your birthday or give you something expensive and not be with you?

A Little Talk about
Jesus and You

1. What would you rather have from Jesus, His love or lots of money?

2. Jesus said He is with us always. Would you rather have that or a castle without Him?

3. Jesus said that we can live with Him in heaven. Would you rather have that or be king over a big country? Why?

Bible Reading: Matthew 6:31-34.

Bible Truth: It is better to have a little and love the Lord than to have much with a messed-up life (Proverbs 15:16).

Prayer: Dear Jesus, give me Your best gifts—Your love, Your home in heaven, and Your presence by my side until I go there to live. Amen.

Don't Burst
Your Balloon

Kent was bragging to his friends. Father heard everything he said.

"I can run faster than anyone in my class," said Kent. "I probably can run faster than anyone in my school. Who knows, maybe I can run faster than anyone in town." Kent didn't stop bragging there either.

When Kent's friends left, Father came into the family room with Kent. "I heard what you told your friends," said Father. "I kept thinking of one word each time you told them how fast you are."

A Little Talk about
Bragging

1. Do you like to hear a friend brag? Why not?

2. Have you bragged about anything this week? Do you think your friends like to hear you brag? Why not?

"Tell me exactly what you told your friends," Father said to Kent.

Kent's face became red. "Aw, don't make me do that," he said.

"Please, go ahead," said Father. "I want you to see something." Kent saw then that Father had a balloon. It had not been blown up yet. "What will Father do with it?" he wondered.

Kent said he could run faster than anyone in his class. Father took the balloon and blew a big puff of air into it.

"Go on," said Father.

Then Kent said he could run faster than anyone in his school. Father blew another big puff of air into the balloon. When Kent said he could run faster than anyone in town, Father blew another puff of air into the balloon.

Suddenly the balloon burst with a loud bang. Kent almost jumped out of his chair.

"Three puffs of bragging and the balloon burst," said Father. "I wonder how many more times you could have bragged before you would have burst with pride."

"I won't do it again," said Kent. "I'm sorry."

A Little Talk about
Jesus and You

1. How is bragging like blowing up a balloon? How many puffs of bragging did it take to blow up the balloon that Father had?

2. What would you say to Kent about bragging? What will you remember the next time you think about bragging?

Bible Reading: Luke 14:8-11.

Bible Truth: Whoever makes himself look big will be made to look little (Luke 14:11).

Prayer: Please remind me of that balloon, dear Lord. Keep me from blowing up my pride. I know You would not be pleased. Amen.

Helping Someone
Who Is Alone

"Oh, no!" said Father. "Look at this! Poor old Mrs. Turnbull fell at home and hurt herself. No one was with her, and she couldn't get to a phone."

Mother looked at the newspaper that Father was reading. "Poor Mrs. Turnbull—if only we had known," said Mother. "Is she all right?"

"Someone found her, and she is better now," he answered. "She is in Memorial Hospital."

Paul looked at the newspaper too. He saw Mrs. Turnbull's picture.

"I go past her house every day on the way home from school," said Paul. "She was lying there hurting when I went by her house, and I didn't even know it." Paul looked so sad that Mother and Father felt sorry for him.

Then Paul smiled. "I have an idea!" he said. "I know how I can help Mrs. Turnbull."

A Little Talk about
Helping

1. Do you feel sorry for Mrs. Turnbull? Why couldn't she get help?

2. What do you think Paul's idea is? Do you have any good ideas about helping Mrs. Turnbull?

"When Mrs. Turnbull gets home, I will stop at her house each day," said Paul. "I will ask her if everything is all right."

Mother and Father both smiled. "That would be a wonderful thing to do," said Father.

"She will look forward to that," said Mother. "That will be the best part of her day. She won't really be alone when you do that."

Paul could hardly wait for Mrs. Turnbull to get home. It would be fun to help her.

A LITTLE TALK about
Jesus and You

1. Why does Jesus want us to help people who cannot help themselves?

2. Is there someone like Mrs. Turnbull you can help? What could you do for that person?

Bible Reading: Matthew 25:34-40.

Bible Truth: Pity the person who falls down and has no one to help him up (Ecclesiastes 4:10).

Prayer: Dear Lord, if there is someone who needs me, help me know what to do. Then help me do it. Amen.

Temper Tantrums and
Broken Towers

Craig had tried six times to put the blocks together. Each time the tower fell down.

The seventh time that the tower fell down, Craig rolled on the floor. He pounded the floor with his fists. And he said some things that good tower-builders should never say.

"Hmm," said Grandmother, "seems to me the tower-builder looks just like his tower."

Craig stopped rolling on the floor. He stopped saying nasty things.

"What do you mean?" Craig asked.

"The Bible tells us about your tower and you. It tells us what happened to your tower and you," said Grandmother.

Craig looked surprised. "It does? What does it say about me and my tower?" he asked.

A Little Talk about

Temper Tantrums

1. Have you ever had a temper tantrum? What happened? How did you feel after you did this?

2. What's wrong with a temper tantrum? Why should boys and girls not have them?

3. If you were Grandmother, what would you say to Craig about temper tantrums?

"Proverbs 25:28 tells us about you and your tower," said Grandmother. "It says that a person who can't control himself is like the walls of a city that are broken down. That's another way of saying that a boy who can't control himself is like his tower that has fallen down."

Craig looked at his tower that had fallen on the floor. It was a mess. He had worked so hard to put it together just right, but now many of the pieces had come apart. It didn't look much like the tower he had planned so carefully.

"I don't want to be like that messed-up tower," said Craig. "I want to be more like the tower before it fell. I'm going to ask Jesus to help me control my temper from now on."

A LITTLE TALK about
Jesus and You

1. Why didn't Craig want to be like his messed-up tower? Would you?

2. What did Craig want Jesus to help him do? Do you want Jesus to help you control your temper? Why not ask Him now?

Bible Reading: Proverbs 25:28.

Bible Truth: A person who has a temper tantrum is like a city with its walls broken down (Proverbs 25:28).

Prayer: Dear Jesus, I don't want to be like a broken wall. I don't want to be like a tower that fell down. Help me control my temper, the way You would. Amen.

The Dragon

"Look at that mean dragon!" said Ralph. He pointed to a big stuffed dragon in the parade. Its teeth were long and sharp, and it had mean-looking eyes. It didn't look kind at all.

"Have you ever met any other dragons?" Father asked.

Ralph looked surprised. Then he began to think. What do you suppose Ralph will say?

A Little Talk about

Being Mean

1. Did the dragon look kind or mean?

2. What do you think Father meant when he asked Ralph if he had met any other dragons? Have you?

3. What do you think Ralph will say to Father? What would you say if you were Ralph?

"I've seen friends who act like mean dragons," said Ralph. "They are cross and angry and try to hurt other people instead of help them."

"What would you like to say to those friends?" Father asked.

"I guess I would like to tell them to stop acting like dragons," said Ralph. "No one wants to be friends with a mean dragon."

"That's good for us to remember too, isn't it?" Father asked.

"Yes, I suppose it is," said Ralph. "Jesus doesn't want us to act like mean old dragons."

A LITTLE TALK about
Jesus and You

1. Why doesn't Jesus want us to act like mean old dragons? Does He ever act that way? If He doesn't, why should we?

2. How should Jesus' friends be? Should we be kind? What would Jesus want?

Bible Reading: 1 Thessalonians 5:15-18.

Bible Truth: Always try to be kind to each other (1 Thessalonians 5:15).

Prayer: Dear Jesus, You are kind and loving and helpful. Let me be more like You each day. Amen.

Be Courteous

"I don't believe it!" said Mother. "Look at that woman cut into the middle of the line!"

Audrey looked at the woman. She couldn't believe it either. Her mother would never do that.

"She should be ashamed of herself," said Audrey. "That's rude. I'd like to tell her that she's rude."

"No, let's not do that," said Mother. "It would only start a quarrel. Perhaps she is in a hurry to get somewhere. We will forgive her, won't we? I can wait another two minutes to pay for my groceries."

A Little Talk about
Being Courteous

1. What would you like to say to that woman who cut into the line at the grocery store? Have you ever seen people do rude things like that?

2. Do you always try to be courteous to other people? What are some special things you can do to be courteous to others? What are some rude things you should not do?

When Audrey and Mother came home and put the groceries away, they sat down at the kitchen table.

"Let's make a list of some courteous things that a girl like you can do," said Mother. "Then let's make a list of rude things that a girl like you should not do."

Audrey and Mother came up with two long lists. Do you suppose they have lists like yours?

A LITTLE TALK about
Jesus and You

1. Why should Christians be courteous? Why would Jesus want that?

2. Think of three Christian men or women whom you like very much. Are they courteous?

3. Think of someone you hope to be like when you grow up. Is that person courteous?

Bible Reading: I Peter 3:8-12.

Bible Truth: Be courteous (I Peter 3:8).

Prayer: Lord, I want to be courteous because I know this will please You and others who watch me. Amen.

"Perhaps a yellow smiling face like this is another way of sending a smile through the mail," said Mother. "Does it make you want to smile too?"

Carol looked at the smiling face again. Then she began to smile. "It does," she said.

"When you smile, it makes a friend want to smile too," said Mother. "But when you frown, it can make your friends sad. Jesus wants His friends to be cheerful, don't you think?"